Would you like to be an animal?

You could be a dog.

You could be a bunny.

You could be a cat.

You could be a bear.

You could be a tiger.

You could be a horse.

You could be a hamster.

You could be an
elephant.

You could be a bird.

You could be a goat.

You could be a frog.

You could be a panda.

You could be a sea horse.

You could be a peacock.

I would like to be an animal.
I would be a turtle!